VIRGINIA READERS

#45

King James I
A King of Many Lands

by Carole Marsh

A Coloring & Activity Book

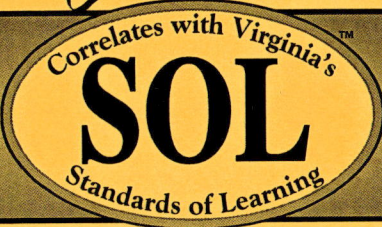

Correlates with Virginia's **SOL** Standards of Learning

A Kid Friendly Biography

VIRGINIA Experience

A Word From the Author!

King James was born King of Scotland. He later became King of England and founder of the first permanent colony in the New World – the colony of Jamestown, Virginia.

Carole Marsh

About the Author...

Carole Marsh is the author of many books about Virginia. She is the creator of The Virginia Experience, which includes books, workbooks, software, stickers, maps, and other products based on the Virginia SOL. You can write to her at carolemarsh@gallopade.com.

Editorial Assistant: Billie Walburn
Graphic Designer: Cecil Anderson

©Carole Marsh/Gallopade International. This book is not reproducible.

Published by GALLOPADE INTERNATIONAL members of:

SHOPA MEMBER
School, Home, & Office Products Association

NSSEA

ASCD

King James I

His father was murdered before James was a year old.

The Ruler Who Made America What It Is Today!

King James was born on June 19, 1566 at Edinburg Castle in Scotland. He was baptized James Charles Stuart.

Starting with the W, cross out every other letter to find out what happened to James' mother, Mary, Queen of Scots.

WSIHUE
EWPACS
HBREIHSEPAHDCEWD!

His mother, Mary, Queen of Scots, was forced to give up the Scottish throne and imprisoned by her cousin Queen Elizabeth I of England. James was only 13 months old. James became King James VI of Scotland when his mother was forced to give up her throne.

James, the boy king, was raised by four tutors. Political leaders took control of Scotland. James' education included learning many languages such as Greek, Latin, Italian, Spanish, French, and English.

Unscramble the words in the sentences to learn more about the foreign languages James learned.

As an _____,
a u d l t

James did not _____ translators
ndee

to _____ business with foreign
od

countries because he could

_____ their languages.
s e p a k

When James was 13, he took over a minor role in ruling Scotland. When James was 15, he was kidnapped by religious leaders who wanted to take control of the country. James escaped a year later.

When James was 23, he married Princess Anne, daughter of the King of Denmark. James and Anne had a long and happy marriage. They had nine children.

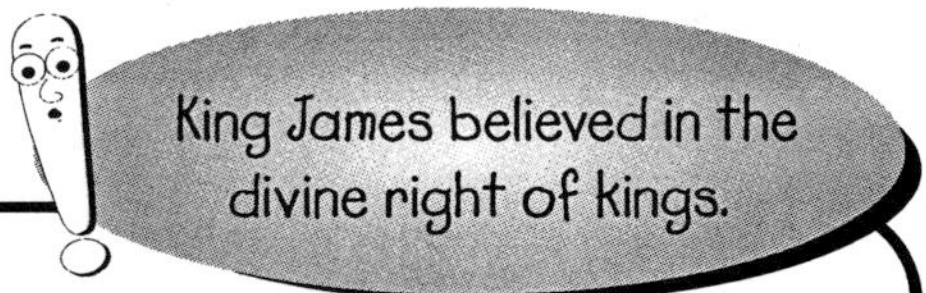

King James believed in the divine right of kings.

Pull apart the sentence below to find out more about the *divine right of kings*.

Itisthebeliefthatkings

gettherighttorulefrom

God,notfromthepeople.

King James and Queen Anne both enjoyed spending lots of money.

In 1603, James' cousin, Queen Elizabeth I of England, died. James took over her throne and became known as King James I of England.

Place a check by the following true statements.

_____ King James was born in Scotland.

_____ His father was killed when James was less than a year old.

_____ His mother was imprisoned when he was 10 years old.

_____ James took over the throne of Denmark in 1603.

English leaders and Catholics did not like him — not because he was a bad king, but because he was Scottish and not Catholic.

James was known as King James I of England and King James VI of Scotland.

In 1606, King James granted a charter to start a colony in the New World. He sent Christopher Newport, John Smith, and 142 settlers to start the colony.

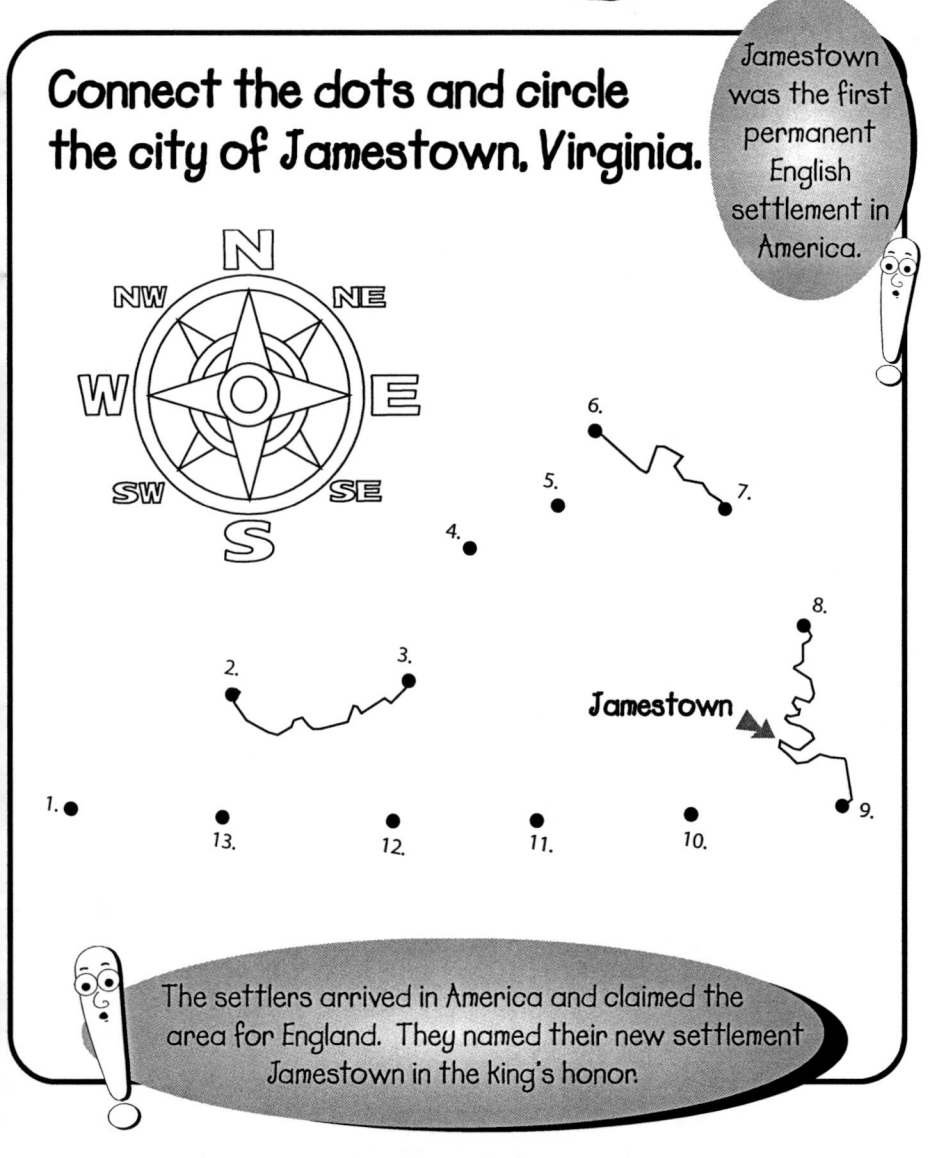

Connect the dots and circle the city of Jamestown, Virginia.

Jamestown was the first permanent English settlement in America.

The settlers arrived in America and claimed the area for England. They named their new settlement Jamestown in the king's honor.

When King James learned that the land in the colony had much to offer, he sent more settlers and doubled the colony's size.

Find the words in the Word Find below.

COLONY   TOBACCO   VIRGINIA

V	O	S	X
P	I	B	E
G	V	R	N
N	E	A	G
I	M	C	L
K	S	I	T
B	S	C	G
H	Y	N	O

King James and Queen Anne loved to hunt. Once when they were hunting, she accidentally shot and killed his favorite dog. To show that he forgave her, King James presented Queen Anne with a large diamond!

John Rolfe, the settler who married Pocahontas, developed a profitable crop in Jamestown. The crop was tobacco. King James did not like the use of tobacco. He said it was "dangerous to the lungs."

KING   JAMES   ENGLISH   ANNE

```
V   E   N   T
N   T   E   O
M   N   U   B
G   A   N   A
I   S   J   C
G   N   U   C
U   Q   I   O
L   O   C   A
```

The English thought of Pocahontas as an Indian "princess."

While in England, Pocahontas became ill with smallpox. She died before she could return to her American homeland.

King James was asked to create an English translation of the Bible. In July 1604, he appointed 24 men to serve on a translation committee. They were the best scholars in the world. The Bible they created is still used today. It's called the King James Version.

Put the events in order.

_____ King James became King of England.

_____ King James grants a charter for a colony in the New World.

_____ King James was born in Scotland.

_____ King James married Princess Anne of Denmark.

While Pocahontas was in England, she met King James. They talked about his translation of the Bible. She impressed King James with how well she could quote from the Bible.

In the last year of his life, King James worried about the settlers being attacked. He also worried about the diseases and hunger that they faced. James put the colony under royal control.

Solve the code below to find out who was attacking the settlers.

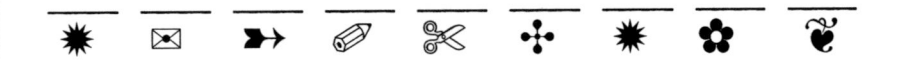

A	B	C	D	E	F	G	H	I	J	K	L	M
✹	❀	✣	♣	➢	♥	❢	❉	✂	◐	☛	✈	✉

N	O	P	Q	R	S	T	U	V	W	X	Y	Z
✿	☆	◆	✡	✏	❦	☎	☙	✚	✖	✍	✠	✓

__ __ __ __ __ __
 ✿ ✹ ☎ ✂ ✚ ➢

__ __ __ __ __ __ __ __ __
 ✹ ✉ ➢ ✏ ✂ ✣ ✹ ✿ ❦

Jamestown continued under royal control for another 150 years until the nation's founding fathers decided to change it — during the American Revolution.

Although King James had set up a strong royal government in Scotland, the English Parliament opposed him ruling as an absolute monarch in England. King James died in 1625. His son Charles I succeeded him.

Color the picture of King James.

Glossary

absolute monarch: a ruler who is not limited by any rules or conditions

foreign: of or from another country

grant: to give what is asked for or wanted

reign: the time a monarch rules

succeed: to come after, to come next, to follow

translator: a person who puts words of a different language into a language someone understands

Pop Quiz!

1. Where was King James born?
   - ○ Scotland
   - ○ England
   - ○ Virginia

2. James was known as King James VI of Scotland and King James I of:
   - ○ Germany
   - ○ England
   - ○ Denmark

3. Which crop did King James dislike?
   - ○ Tobacco
   - ○ Corn
   - ○ Wheat

4. Who was Kings James' wife?
   - ○ Mary
   - ○ Anne
   - ○ Rebecca

5. Which settlement in the New World was named for King James?
   - ○ Richmond
   - ○ Jamestown
   - ○ Jamesville

©Carole Marsh/Gallopade International/800-536-2GET/www.virginiaexperience.com
This page is not reproducible.